Why Your Skin is Beautiful

Millie and Suzie Learn about their Skin

written by
Samantha Harris & Devon Scott
with Dr. Kenya Hameed

illustrated by
Harriet Rodis

To my nieces and nephews
-SH

To everyone that always believed in me
-DS

ISBN 978-1-7352163-1-7 (Paperback)

MillieandSuzie.com

A Note to Parents and Caregivers
on Speaking with Kids about Racism

For many families, talking about racism is an uncomfortable topic. Children DO see color, regardless of whether it is explicitly discussed. Racism is systemic and embedded in the fabric of our society. It impacts the education we receive, where we live, how much money we make and how we are treated and perceived by others. By not talking about it, we unintentionally contribute to its existence and maintain its hold on our society. As parents and caregivers, be sure to give children concrete information about what racism is, examples of racist comments and behaviors as well as empower them to speak up when they witness or experience racism themselves. A child's potential is limitless, let's ensure we build a future that doesn't hinder their greatness.

-Kenya Hameed, PsyD
Clinical Neuropsychologist

"No one is born hating another person because of the color of his skin, or his background, or his religion. People must learn to hate, and if they can learn to hate, they can be taught to love, for love comes more naturally to the human heart than its opposite."
- Nelson Mandela

"I really hope the doctor is able to help me feel less itchy." Millie says. Millie, Suzie and Mommy are sitting in the waiting room of the doctor's office. Millie's arms have been really itchy lately and now she has a rash. Mommy decided to bring Millie to Dr. Stewart to see if she could help.

"Me too," says Suzie.

"Millie, Dr. Stewart is ready to see you now," the nurse says.

Millie, Suzie and Mommy walk into Dr. Stewart's office. Dr. Stewart is already in the room and waiting to greet them. "Hello, nice to meet you. My name is Dr. Stewart. Can you tell me your names?"

"My name is Suzie. This is my big sister Millie and our Mommy. Millie's arms are very itchy. Can you fix them?"

"Nice to meet you Suzie and Millie," Dr. Stewart says. "Millie, I am sorry to hear that your arms have been bothering you. Why don't you sit on the table so that I can take a look at them."

Mommy picks Millie up and places her on the table. Dr. Stewart takes a look at Millie's arms. She realizes why Millie has been itchy and knows a way that she can help her.

"Well Millie, it seems as though you have eczema. Eczema is when the skin gets irritated and then becomes itchy. I am going to give your Mommy a special cream that should help this get better."

"Thank you so much, Dr. Stewart," Mommy says. "You are such a great dermatologist."

"What is a derma-toe-lo-logist?" Suzie asks.

"A dermatologist is a doctor that helps people with different problems that they have with their skin. I also teach children about different ways that they can protect their skin; like making sure to put on sunscreen when they go to the beach."

"Our skin does such a great job of protecting us. The skin is the biggest organ that we have, and it is responsible for covering all of the other organs in our body. The skin is made of 2 layers, the dermis, and the epidermis."

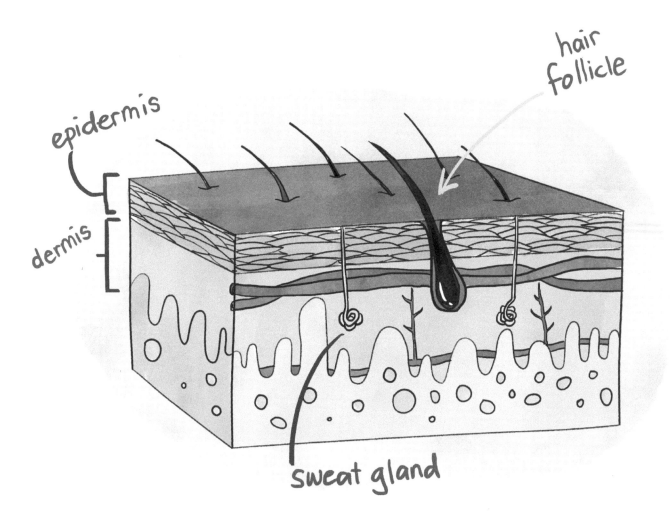

epidermis

dermis

hair follicle

sweat gland

"But what is skin made of and why does it come in so many different colors?" Suzie asks.

"Great question Suzie! Our skin is made up of many tiny building blocks that we cannot see. These building blocks are called cells.

Skin cells make a product called melanin. Some people's cells make more melanin than others, but it is important to remember that all skin is the same no matter what color it is," says Dr. Stewart.

cells →

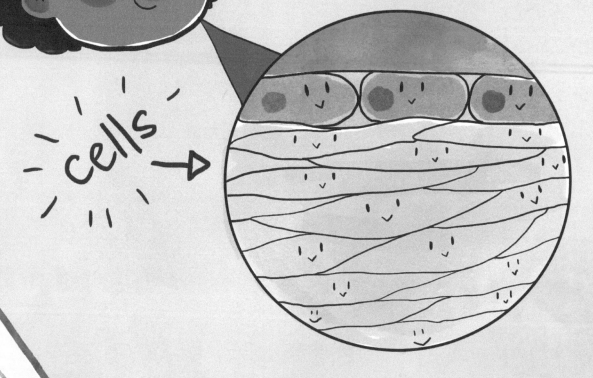

"Dr. Stewart is right girls, all skin is the same no matter the color," Mommy says. "Some people do not think that all skin is the same. They treat people differently and unfairly because of the color of their skin. This is wrong."

"But why would anyone want to be mean to someone just because of their skin color?" Suzie asked.

"Well Suzie, there is something call race. A race is a group of people who have somethings in common such as their skin color and hair. They are many different races. Some people believe that one race is better than another. This is called racism. But I want you to know that each race is special, equal and important."

"When racism is in someone's heart, they might do terrible things like not invite someone of a different skin color to play with them or call someone mean names because of how their skin or hair looks,"

"Treating groups of people unfairly because of the color of their skin is wrong. If someone treats you that way, I want you to know that it is not your fault. You did nothing wrong. Your skin is perfect just the way it is," Dr. Stewart says.

"What Dr. Stewart is saying is very important. Although racism has been around in our country for over a hundred years, it is not something that we are born with. Some kids are taught racism from grown-ups, while others learn racism through what they see in everyday life."

"Well if racism is something that is learned, can it be un-learned?" Millie asks.

"That's a great question, Millie. Many people throughout our history, like Martin Luther King Jr., Rosa Parks, John Lewis and Colin Kaepernick, have worked towards putting an end to racism. It is a hard thing to do and we need everyone's help, both big and small,"

"If we see someone treating others unfairly, we should tell them to stop, and find an adult who can help," Mommy says.

"I understand," says Millie. "I would never want anyone to be treated differently because of their skin color. That's awful. Thank you so much for giving my Mommy the cream for my arms Dr. Stewart and for teaching us all about our skin."

"You're welcome!" says Dr. Stewart.
"I want you to always remember
that your skin is beautiful, Millie!"

"Hey! What about my skin?" says
Suzie.

"Your skin is beautiful too, Suzie,"
Dr. Stewart says with a smile.

"Dr. Stewart, I am really happy that you can help Millie's arms stop feeling so itchy and that you are Millie's derma-toe-lo-logist," says Suzie.

"No, Dr. Stewart is a dermatologist Suzie. You said it wrong," Millie says.

"It's okay Suzie; I am happy that I'm Millie's dermatologist too!" Dr. Stewart says with a smile.

Millie and Suzie's Career Spotlight!

Dr. Susan C. Taylor

is an African American female dermatologist from Pennsylvania. She founded the Skin of Color Society in 2004. This society helps dermatologists provide excellent care to their patients who have skin of color. We thank Dr. Taylor for all that she is doing in the field of dermatology!

Look out for our next learning adventure with Millie and Suzie, coming soon!

CPSIA information can be obtained
at www.ICGtesting.com
Printed in the USA
LVHW072347271020
669935LV00002B/21